The Housed Sun

Poetry and Prayers

The Housed Sun

Poetry and Prayers

Valerie Boone

For information on the content of this book, email boonev900@gmail.com

Scriptures used in this publication are quoted from the King James Version - Bible in Public Domain; and the New International Version (NIV) Holy Bible, New International Version®, NIV® Copyright ©1973, 1978, 1984, 2011 by Biblica, Inc.® Used by permission.

WrightStuf *Consulting, LLC*

www.wrightstuf.com
info@wrightstuf.com

Printed in the United States of America

Acknowledgments

What a wonderful God we serve! Father God, because of your grace and Love. I am forever indebted to you and owe my life to you. I am overwhelmed with thankfulness for you, and the purpose you ordained within my life, and the gifts of written love languages to be shared with your people. It's all for your glory. Hallelujah!!! I receive this new life that has sprung forth within me that you have freely given. I love you so, Abba Father, because you first loved me!

To my spiritual dad, Pops, pastor, Apostle Joseph L. Young, of House of Prayer for All People, Church International, thank you for empowering and uplifting me through your words of encouragement, teachings, prayers, and prophetic revelations spoken over my life and my family. I am so grateful to have you as a part of my life! I have grown fond of you and your jokes! You are the example of how Kingdom children are to live a consecrated life in Him, KING Jesus, that our region and this old world needs. Pops, you truly have the heart of the Father and a love for his people! I love you, Pops! God bless you always!

To my daughter, Jocelyn O. Brown, who pushes me to speak well and to be a better me! This young girl is very mature and advanced in age! Thank you, and God bless you, Sweetie! Mommy loves you! I am forever grateful for my family, who has been by my side through it all and shared their kindness and love towards me! I love you all! God bless!

Apostle-Prophet Darryl Evans and his lovely wife, Intercessor Norchell Evans; Pastor Jonathan Brown and his beautiful wife, Prophetess Ashley Brown; Minister Tracy Williams; Sister Jacquesha Stanton; and Sister Kima Prince; and several others that have spoken life unto me, concerning the heart of Father. I am so thankful for God's blessings, teachings, and prophetic words that you all have shared through prayers, spending time with me, and listening to me! I love and thank each one of you! God bless!

To Sister Skyye Howe, this dynamic woman of God, who helped me birth my second book of poetry and prayers. I am truly honored to have had your divine help from heaven! Thank you so much for your patience, love, and support and for speaking life back into me! You are truly a woman after God's own heart! Your love and compassion for God's people are so overwhelming with the love of the Father! You are amazing! I love you, Sister Skyye! God bless!

A special thanks to Apostle-Prophet Tavares Tate and his ministry, Team Jesus of Atlanta, Georgia! I am so thankful for the life you live before God's people, for being the vessel God ordained to plant and water, and for bringing forth growth in his children! This book would not have been so if God had not allowed me to put feet to the urgency of his revelation spoken through you! I love you, Prophet Tate, and your ministry! God bless!

Table of Contents

Introduction

Introduction

"The Housed Sun" is about covering up my wanting to live a life of normalcy. So many of God's children have gone through struggles of rejection, past hurt, pain, and much more. This causes one to be judgmental of their own strengths and insecurities. Going back and forth with bad habits, not growing, losing passion, and not walking with God. My past attitudes and behaviors were not aligned with God's Kingdom. I found myself blocking the sun from shining on my life, being housed in ways that caused me to revisit things from which I was delivered.

"The Housed Sun" is a book of personal testimonials written through poetry and prayers of my spiritual journey. I don't know what you have housed, but it's time to pull the curtains back over whatever you may have suffered over the years. Your daily deliverance begins now.

"This Rejection"

Daily Deliverance One

Poetry

Scripture Meditation: Isaiah 53:3

"He was despised and rejected by humankind, a man of suffering, and familiar with pain. Like one from whom people hide their faces, He was despised, and we held him in low esteem."

SIGH, I flow into the deep to speak of how it feels. I hope this poetry helps you see what I have been dealing with for years:

This rejection is the season of my scars and the reflection of what's been happening. You can never see the bigger picture of what you face and learn. The only thing you will see is this rejection is killing me.

Quote: "Rejection is the form of your voice that has never been heard of."

It's tingling like an allergic reaction of being stung by a bee. How long will it be for my deliverance to come? For my healing and to be made WHOLE?

O Lord, my God, let the chains be broken off of me. I want to be free once and for all! This rejection hurts so much. To be rejected by loved ones, I have become numb from the pain of evil speaking, lies, and their residues. This rejection shall cease to exist in my life and the lives of my loved ones. In the name of Jesus!

But wait, I didn't get to the root of the problem. I faced insecurities. I beat myself up because I thought I wasn't chosen, and I've been feeling like this rejection has torn my whole life down. In fact, I stop smiling, I stop praising, and I start drowning. What am I to do? Is God there? Is He true? So many questions. The editing of my voice is cracking. No tears, but I'm screaming inside from this rejection.

"Hope and Surrender"

Daily Deliverance Two

Prayer

Scripture Meditation: Romans 5:5

"Now hope does not disappoint, because the love of God has been poured out in our hearts by the Holy Spirit who was given to us."

YES, Abba, Father!

I say yes to your perfect will for my life, LORD God! I want to be set free and made whole! I am FREE! The flesh wants to be pleased all night long. My flesh has fixed, groans, moans, and cries out to be happy. It rages like the wild waves in the ocean when stirred. How long, O' LORD, will it overtake me?

Come my LORD and rescue me from the one that tempts my soul and even me, that one that craves fleshly desires that are impure. She wants to be satisfied. She cries out to draw the attention of men, being seductive with her eyes and calm demeanor. I am divorcing this flesh of mine. My past tries to hold me back and calls to me. I will not look back nor answer its familiar voices.

My flesh, you shall die, but my Spirit and Soul shall live! My body belongs to the one who created it in His own image! The one who prevails over all! The one who empties me daily and fills me with His Spirit!

I shall not die, but I shall live life, and I shall proclaim the works of the LORD! I belong to the LORD my God, thee Almighty!

"Change My Mindset"

Daily Deliverance Three

Poetry

Scripture Meditation: Isaiah 43:19

"Remember not the former things, nor consider the things of old. Behold, I am doing a new thing; now it springs forth, do you not perceive it? I will make a way in the wilderness and rivers in the desert."

Change my mindset, O God, so that I may perform with grace and with the anointing you gave. I have found myself being tapped into the familiar.

Here I go again! That old mindset, that familiar, that past coming after me. Woman, when will you change that mindset of yours?

Let go and let God have His way in you, Woman of God! All of you! Allow the Father to pour His Spirit into you so that you may grow and prosper.

Do not look back! Keep moving forth. You will make it through. Trust in the LORD your God to bring you out and make you WHOLE!

In the Mighty name of Jesus! Hallelujah!!!

"Young Woman"

Daily Deliverance Four

Prayer

Scripture Meditation: Song of Solomon 3:5

"Promise me o woman of Jerusalem by the gazelles and wild deer, not to awaken love until the time is right."

Dear God,

Help us wait on the right love. Don't let us get impatient and do the wrong thing, for we know the consequences of getting outside your will. God gives us the strength to keep our eyes on you, to keep our legs closed, and to keep your commandments to wait until marriage.

Father, while temptation will come, let us see past the mask of falseness. Let us see the devour before it comes and let us shift into the spirit realm to notify the devil that he is defeated, and we will not fall into his traps to be snared. Let purity be our portion. Let your light shine through us so we can seek the right Love, the right chance, and the right directions.

O, young woman, don't be desperate for a mate. Stay at Jesus' feet for the right voice to speak.

O, Young woman, continue to practice celibacy, your life is worth waiting for, and your body is worth keeping.

O, young woman, don't dismiss prayer, don't go astray to be in the bed. Allow the Holy Spirit to lead you into the guidance of something real and something true.

O, young woman, you are the precious jewel. Keep yourself hidden in Christ. The love you need will soon find you.

In Jesus' name, we pray. Amen.

"King on the Cross"

Daily Deliverance Five

Poetry

Scripture Meditation: Luke 23:30

"Then they will begin to say to the mountains, "Fall on us!" and to the hills. Cover us!"

God is the King on the cross who can move mountains, who can set the captives free.

God is the King on the cross who died for all our sins.

God is the King on the cross who was willing to take a nail in His hand and thorns in His crown.

While seeking Jesus, know that he's still saving us all from sins, bondage, trauma, and selfishness.

God is the King on the cross who is heading for victory, while we have already won, He has suffered the one and only perfect one.

God is the King on the cross that has replaced the dictation of other idols, other voices, and people who refuse to help see the growth.

God is the King on the cross. The only reference you need to be free, to see, to be healed, to see the miracle sounds and wonders.

Oh, how Great the King can be if we will just obey and respect what He did for us all on the cross.

Don't be afraid of the King on the cross, don't focus on the cloudy days, don't select what you want. Everything is laid out at the cross.

"Back To You"

Daily Deliverance Six

Prayer

Scripture Meditation: Zechariah 1:3

"Therefore, say to them, 'Thus says the Lord of hosts, "Return to Me," declares the Lord of hosts, "that I may return to you," says the Lord of hosts.

Dear Sovereign, One,

Help me to ignore the voices that have called out to me, there are so many, but none were from you. God, forgive me for straying away from home. O' how I have missed my Father's presence and His Love. I don't know why I left you. I don t know why I stopped caring, but in this moment, I need you.

My Spirit is all tired out and thirsty for my Abba Father. Help me get back to you. I have lost my way. The laughter of my enemies surrounds me on all sides. Protect me and shield me.

Sometimes, I don't know how to escape this madness. I am crying out to you, Jesus. I am feeling alone and scared, and I need to get back to you. I am making my way back to you!

I miss sitting at your feet to hear your voice again and feel your warm embrace touching my soul. Sigh, the tears can't stop falling. I love you, Daddy. I am coming and making my way back to you. And this time, I will never leave again.

"I Will Arise"

Daily Deliverance Seven

Poetry

Scripture Meditation: *Genesis 21:18*
"Arise, lift up the lad, and hold him in thine hand; for I will make him a great nation."

The Son had shone His light into the dark places I had once embraced and lived as a slave to the upending of my desires.

As the sun rises in the morning, so will my soul live and arise in the light of the Almighty Son, Jesus Christ.

I will fear no more of what man can do or say to me. For I am a child of the Most High surrendering my will for His perfect will.

I WILL ARISE. I will shine as a light for all to see, all for my Father's Glory. No longer will I live ashamed, for my life is not hidden, and my Father who breathed life into me.

I will arise, I will arise. Hallelujah, I will arise for your Glory! Thank you, Jesus, for arising me even when I feel like a failure! It's time to rise and shine!

"No Time to Waste"

Daily Deliverance Eight

Prayer

Scripture Meditation: *Roman 12:2*

"Do not be conformed to this world, but be transformed by the renewal of your mind, that by testing you may discern what is the will of God, what is good and acceptable and perfect."

Dear Heavenly Father,

Give me (us) the wisdom to not waste time in this season. The instructions you give us don't let our flesh fight against what you are doing and excelling in what you want to be done. No time to waste in our living, no time to waste in our dreaming, no time to waste in our monies, no time to waste in our daily bread, no time to waste in our fellowshipping, no time to waste in our forgiving, no time to waste in our giving, no time to waste in our sharing, no time to waste with salvation, not time to waste loving on our children, no time to waste to hold grudges in our hearts.

God, we thank you for loving us and giving us time on this earth to do what you have called us to do. Let us learn and prepare with the time you have gifted us with. Time is powerful, time is short, and time is of the essence. God help us, show us, and give us the wisdom to not waste your precious time. In Jesus' name. Amen.

"Foolish No More"

Daily Deliverance Nine

Poetry

Scripture Meditation: Ephesians 5:2

"and walk in love, just as Christ also loved you and gave Himself up for us, an offering and a sacrifice to God as a fragrant aroma."

Beloved, be about your Father's business. Focus on Him. No more foolishness, no more doubting or choosing.

Call upon His name. He is ready and will come to your rescue, my beloved. There is no time in wandering, no time in pondering, no time to be foolish.

It is time to hear God. He is saying, I am with you, guiding your every move. Listen to my instructions; they will bring life to you. Don't quit, don't give up.

Look to the hills from whence cometh your help. I am with you, my beloved, be foolish no more.

Remember what you have, keep being steady in my name, and keep learning to be sane. You have done it your way long enough, beloved.

Come back to me where you will see, be assured, and be free. Receive my Love and correction now that you may have strength and power to carry out my plan for the perfect will in your life.

I have loved you with everything in me. I am always with you. Be foolish no more. Love, your Abba Father.

"Resting in your Arms"

Daily Deliverance Ten

Prayer

Scripture Meditation: Mark 6:31

"Then, because so many people were coming and going that they did not even have a chance to eat, he said to them, "Come with me by yourselves to a quiet place and get some rest."

Dear Yahweh,

I am coming to you with a heart of worries, stress, and anxiety. Resting in your arms is very important to me. Thank you for showing me how to run to you when the burdens overwhelm me and try to take over my life.

Let me rest in your arms when lies are told, the money is low, and times are hard. Let me rest in your arms when sickness tries to take over my body and the flour is running low in the pantry. God, you know all, see all, and have the answers.

God, your arms are made for us all to fit in. I just need to rest in your arms because life can be a bit overwhelming. We trust that you have the answers we need to live a fruitful, steady, and comfortable life.

Who wouldn't want to serve a God like you? Jesus, you are the truth, the way, and the life. Thank you, Father, for letting me rest in your arms.

"To Be Loved"

Daily Deliverance Eleven

Poetry

Scripture Meditation: *Jeremiah 1:8*
""Do not be afraid of them, For I am with you to deliver
you," declares the
Lord."

Love is deeper than a feeling. Love speaks aloud, crying for someone to embrace her. Love is never ashamed of you but accepts you as you are. Love will come to your rescue and shelter you from the storm.

Love longs to show how deeply she cares for you. Wanting more of you. Love will give her time to you, and when you are lonely, love will lift you up. Love is kind and eager to share. Love will never mistreat you. Love will show you the way to a better life. Love will never lie on you. Love is not jealous. Love secures the broken you.

In fact, Love can rescue you from all your troubles. To be loved is to know God and to surrender your all. And I just wanted to be loved by our Father, who is the epitome and King of Agape Love. Its unfailing Love is forever and ever.

"Wars For Me"

Daily Deliverance Twelve

Prayer

Scripture Meditation: Psalm 16:8

"I have set the Lord always before me; because he is at my right hand, I shall not be shaken."

Dear God,

I thank you for warring for me. You have kept me alive as your angels have kept a guard on and over my life. God, when you war for me, you show me that your Love is real, your joy is still, and your hands work unchangeable miracles that leave me wondering how and why you did that for me.

God, thank you for all you do for my family and me. God, when you war for me, I feel so protected, so grateful, so humbled, and so changed. I will still be waddling while you are warring for me. If I have never encountered anything from you, I don't take your presence lightly. I understand that with you, I can do all things through Christ that strengthens me. You told me that life can be a breeze if I let you war for me. I trust you, love you, and adore who you are in my life.

The seasons and times are trying, but I am hanging in there with you. God, you are the air I breathe, the solace I need to stay in my rightful place. The Bible says you will fight my battle, and I will let you do just that.

"Joy Is Coming"

Daily Deliverance Thirteen

Poetry

Scripture Meditation: Romans 15:13
"Now may the God of hope fill you with all joy and peace in believing, that you may abound in hope by the power of the Holy Spirit."

The world shows no sign of joy coming but more of destruction and unhappiness to one another. The enemy you see today will be no more; joy is coming. Joy is coming.

Stay strong and hold on. This pain you feel will be no more; joy is coming. Joy is coming, healing is awaiting you, and you will be whole in Jesus' name.

This doubt that you can't seem to shake; joy is coming. Joy is coming.

God is with you and will not leave you. This lack you have been facing; joy is coming. Joy is coming.

So many years of being dried up, but the water is about to flow like streams. This pillar of salt will not cause you to look back. Move forward and bounce back; joy is coming. Joy is coming.

Beloved, remember that you are an overcomer. You will conquer, and you will win. Come receive your joy from the Almighty King.

"I Need You More"

Daily Deliverance Fourteen

Prayer

Scripture Meditation: Psalm 1:2

"But his delight is in the law of the LORD, and on his law, he meditates day and night."

Dear Heavenly Father,

I need more of you. I receive your Spirit, O God. This is my cry. I cannot make it without you. I need more of you; I chose you.

I need more of you in my prayer life, more of you in my devotional time, more of you as a mother, and more of you as a sister. I need more of you as a friend. I need more of you as a neighbor.

Strengthen my heart. Oh, God. Change my mindset and purify my soul. I am a conqueror. I am who you say I am.

Lord, I need you more. The time we spend is the highlight of our day. Show us how to live off your mercy and grace.

God, I truly need more of you in my desperate time of going low, choosing the wrong routes, and flowing. I need more of you to help show others the way; to be used for your Glory and name's sake.

God, I need more of you to help my dreams and goals come alive, so I can thrive and come out of hiding. Lord, I need more of you to pivot me to the top of the mountains to get all you have for me.

"Smile, Sister"

Daily Deliverance Fifteen

Poetry

Scripture Meditation: Psalm 126:2-3

"Our mouths were filled with laughter, our tongues with songs of joy. Then it was said among the nations, "The Lord has done great things for them." The Lord has done great things for us, and we are filled with joy."

The pain you have left and walked in for some years seems as if God and nobody cares. Smile, sister.

Don't worry about the times of not being noticed; recompense will be your portion.

The mind battles come suddenly, but you can still smile and fight to live wholeheartedly.

It all seems to be a reality, as if that's the only way to escape your troubles.

A smile a day lessens the depression and anxiety that flows through your mind daily.

Sister, the devil has lied to you. You are loved; you are worthy of love.

God cares for you; you are never alone. Smile, sister, and hold on.

Remember, the Joy of the Lord is your strength. Don't give up, and don't give in. Chase God to keep smiling over and over again. Smile, Sis. ☺

"Raped"

Daily Deliverance Sixteen

Prayer

Scripture Meditation: Romans 12:19
"Never take your own revenge, beloved, but leave room for the wrath of God, for it is written, "Vengeance is Mine, I will repay," says the Lord."

Dear Almighty One,

Help me not to focus on the enemy attacks of being raped. I have survived the worst, and he comes back to demolish my faith.

The perversion inside tries to take over my life, but I have the strength to fight what's not right. At one point in time, I have failed to his schemes. You raped me; you blinded me into more hurt and more wounds.

God help me get over this as I prepare myself to be scarred for the choices I made. God, I know you are the way of life, so I choose to sacrifice my body to live right.

I will not let you continue to rape me as if I am some piece of trash on the streets. You have seduced me and told me that my body needed to be filled with a thrill. I chased after it with my flesh and the things of the world. It caused you to rape me more.

No more will I settle for less of anything. God has rescued me from the rape of the enemy. I am now free and living out my transparency.

"What Does Love Have to Do With It"

Daily Deliverance Seventeen

Poetry

Scripture Meditation: 1 Corinthians 13:4-5
"Love is patient, Love is kind. It does not envy, it does not boast, it is not proud. It does not dishonor others, it is not self-seeking, it is not easily angered, it keeps no record of wrongs."

What does Love have to do with it.... A Broken Heart, A Crushed Spirit, A Bitter Soul.

Love had everything to do with it!

Love died on the Cross, and Rose up for you.

Love Interceded for you when you did not know what to say in prayer.

Love walked on water to give you that same power to tread over scorpions and serpents.

Love always had and will forever love you when you were cursed and rejected by everyone else.

Love chastened after you when you wanted the love of others to love you the same.

Love had been there all along, protecting, caring, and warring on your behalf.

Love had never left your side; you had needed to look up to the Father in Heaven.

Love carried you when you were weak and wanted to give up.

Love has everything to do with it.... Love WINS! Your life is in the Potter's Hands! Don't give up! You will WIN.

"Fear, You Are Defeated"

Daily Deliverance Eighteen

Poetry

Scripture Meditation: Isaiah 41:10

"Fear not, for I am with you; be not dismayed, for I am your God; I will strengthen you, I will help you, I will uphold you with my righteous right hand."

Fear is at the door again, knocking and trying to get in!

Fear leave. You are not welcome here anymore!

Fear says, "I once lived here before, and you welcomed me in! I have returned to live in this old familiar place."

No, not so, and not this time, and never ever again will I allow this!

Jesus rescued me once and for all, and I no longer have to live a defeated life!

Jesus won the victory on the cross and now intercedes for me.

Fear leave! You are never welcomed here again!

You have been replaced, rejected, and removed with power, love, and a sound mind!

Fear says, "Let me in to test and see!"

Never will I, Valerie Vernett Boone, let you disrupt and disturb this temple of God!

I am a servant of the LORD my God, and only Him will I serve!

The LORD, my God, rebuke thee!!!

Fear screams aloud as he is cast into the outer darkness of hades!

To God be the Glory!

Glory be to God! HALLELUJAH!!!

"Die Flesh"

Daily Deliverance Nineteen

Prayer

Scripture Meditation: Luke 9:23
"And He was saying to them all, "If anyone wishes to come after Me, he must deny himself, and take up his cross daily and follow Me.

Dear Sovereign One,

Allow me to die to the flesh. The flesh has its way of showing out and giving me the wrong motives. I vow to keep my body in purity and wait if it pleases you.

You have helped me make it out of sin, fornication, and so many other ungodly things; I am grateful for that. I am thankful that you still choose to use me despite my sins.

Dying to the flesh is hard. Flesh likes to feel and hold things. I would say that with time comes wisdom. Thank you for putting people in my way to help me get the things I needed done.

God, you have helped me do what's right, and I want to help others do what's right. God give me the strategy and tools to die to flesh every time it craves for the wrong things and people.

God, you have told me over and over that with life comes instruction, so let me live the instructions of what you think and not what I think.

I understand the consequences of what will happen if I don't die to the flesh. Help me stay alive with your obedience, and flow how you see fit in Jesus' name. Amen.

"No Ishmael"

Daily Deliverance Twenty

Poetry

Scripture Meditation: *Genesis 25:16*
"These [are] the sons of Ishmael, and these [are] their names,
by their towns, and by their castles; twelve princes according
to their nations."

I am no Ishmael. You turned your back on me. Your own flesh and blood, I didn't do anything to you. I am no Ishmael.

I was born and forgotten about, and you deserted me. But little did I know the one who created and filled me with His Spirit when you tried to kill me. I am no Ishmael.

As years went by and learning of a Savior, a Royal Priest, the Deliverer who saved me, I accepted His Love and made a vow to the King, one and true Lord Jesus Christ, to live for Him. I am no Ishmael.

I am the daughter of Jesus, who has set me free from that type of environment. I have shifted the scenery of my life to be all I need to be for God. You told me that if I continue to seek you, I will have your focus, your promises, and the Love to stand when others treat me like an Ishmael.

I am no Ishmael; I am the breath of fresh air that breathes life into others as God shows me the way. Glory, Hallelujah! at

"Suddenly It Came To Pass"

Daily Deliverance Twenty One

Poetry

Scripture Meditation: 2 Corinthians 4:17-18
"For our light affliction, which is but for a moment, is working for us a far more exceeding and eternal weight of Glory, [18] while we do not look at the things which are seen, but at the things which are not seen. For the things which are seen are temporary, but the things which are not seen are eternal."

Things I desire to do, I believe that God will suddenly bring to pass. The anguish of waiting to be free and for manifestation to take place as I wait freely. My heart begins to bubble for Jesus because I know soon everything will come to pass suddenly.

I turned from God because I thought I could do it or be better. Not so. God has helped me climb the ladder. I quickly learned that my way could never work without you. For you know all things before they come to pass, and Father God, I surrender to you, and I will not turn back this time. I will trust the flight that you will have for me to land on. I will trust the journey in which I stand because I know it will suddenly come to pass someday. Amen!

"Rejoice"

Daily Deliverance Twenty Two

Prayer

Scripture Meditation: Philippians 4:4

Rejoice in the Lord always. I will say it again: Rejoice."

Dear Jesus,

I will dance again and rejoice in my faith. My Father didn't forsake me or leave me. I will praise His Holy Name forever and ever.

He lifted me up when I was weak and stumbled without knowing my way. My heart smiles as I think of His goodness. His light overshadows the darkness that once held me captive. I am free, and I will rejoice in Him always.

God, you are a God that never disappoints. You have allowed me to rejoice in the midst of the trials and tests. When I can fully rejoice, I am reminded all over again why life makes sense. I can shout, cry, and be who I am in your presence without being judged but freely rejoice for all you have done for me.

"The Housed Sun"

Daily Deliverance Twenty Three

<u>Poetry</u>

Scripture Meditation: Amos 8:9

"It will come about in that day," declares the Lord God, That I will make the sun go down at noon. And make the earth dark in broad daylight."

Like a prisoner chained behind bars, you allowed the enemy to silence your voice. You, my beloved, were never made to be silenced. Although you are the housed sun, you can still shine through dark days. You are the light in the world, the salt of the earth. For the true King and His righteousness brings the sunlight of praises of God and to speak His truth.

The enemy far too long had His way with you. Being that you are the housed sun, don't dim your light. Open up the curtains to blind Him and show Him out. Trust in God, and He will show the peace to your piece of dysfunction.

No longer will I have the time to sit housed and not allow the sun to shine so others can see, so others can glean, and so others can believe. I am the housed sun that got raped, I prostituted, I suffered rejection, I made myself available to madness. God helped me to get out of the housed sun of not knowing who I was and who I am. I cherished the time I was housed.

I got a chance to seek God's Glory, His Love, and His full permission to be used as the "Sun."

Conclusion

This book of prayer and poetry, "The Housed Sun," is about a woman of God that once lived in Him, walked with Him, sought after Him, and praised Him; but then became silent. She started to believe the lies told about her, ashamed, disappointed with her poor decisions and abused by the enemy. She battled in secret; she bottled up rejections, pains, hurts, unforgiveness, and a lack of confidence in herself and God. Although she knew the truth and once walked in it, she had allowed the enemy to toy with her. Because of her weakness in mind and body, she revisited her old self and stopped chasing after Abba. This Woman of God begins to lose her vision and focus on the Kingdom of God.

She withdraws from God, family, friends, and the church. The anxiety attacks had started out small but soon became more frequent and stronger, especially during the pandemic. She found herself wandering as a lost sheep, depressed, stopped feeding on His Word, and even stopped praying. There were times that she could feel death surrounding her.

Now, she says to herself, *The devil, and this world, loose your hold on me, for I am a daughter of the KING, the MOST HIGH; and I am not to be played with!!!* My light is breaking forth again, and this time to stay forever, and I am who you say I am, LORD, God! I am a bright light to be seen and glorify your holy name! And I receive your grace and mercy. I owe my life to you because of your great Love. I will be free and live the life you gave me to share with others.

I hope whoever is reading this book of prayers and poetry that God will give you a new revelation on your life that brings about a change, and you will be set free! Hallelujah!!! It Is So!!!

Psalm 23:3 He restoreth my soul; he leadeth me in the paths of righteousness for his name's sake. This will be my testimony; to walk with God, talk with him and praise/worship him forever and ever.